United States Government Accountability Office

Report to the Committee on Foreign Relations, U.S. Senate

I0410917

June 2014

COMBATING TERRORISM

State Department Can Improve Management of East Africa Program

GAO Highlights

Highlights of GAO-14-502, a report to the Committee on Foreign Relations, U.S. Senate

COMBATING TERRORISM

State Department Can Improve Management of East Africa Program

Why GAO Did This Study

Terrorism in East Africa has remained a concern of the United States since 1998, when al Qaeda bombed U.S. embassies in Kenya and Tanzania. As part of its efforts to address this threat, State launched PREACT in 2009 as a program for long-term engagement and capacity building in East Africa. PREACT—which focuses on countering terrorist threats, including al Shabaab, an al Qaeda affiliate based in Somalia—is managed by State's Bureau of African Affairs and provides assistance in a region composed of 12 partner countries.

GAO was asked to examine PREACT, including (1) the role it plays in U.S. counterterrorism assistance to East Africa, (2) the extent to which funds allocated for PREACT since 2009 have been disbursed, and (3) the extent to which State considers key factors in managing PREACT. GAO reviewed agency documents and interviewed U.S. officials in Washington, D.C., and in Germany, Djibouti, Ethiopia, and Uganda.

What GAO Recommends

GAO recommends that the Secretary of State improve the management of the PREACT initiative by taking steps to improve the documentation of key factors considered and by routinely collecting activity and funding information. State agreed with all three recommendations and stated that it is taking steps to address them.

View GAO-14-502. For more information, contact Charles Michael Johnson, Jr., 202-512-7331, JohnsonCM@gao.gov.

What GAO Found

State Department's (State) Partnership for Regional East Africa Counterterrorism (PREACT) supports U.S. counterterrorism efforts in East Africa. PREACT's five goals focus on improving partner nations' military capacity, rule of law, border security, ability to counter violent extremism, and ability to counter terrorist financing. PREACT has funded activities such as providing training for terrorist investigation techniques for Somali police, new communications equipment for the Ethiopian military, and computer literacy to teachers working with at-risk youth in Kenya. PREACT assistance is in addition to other U.S. counterterrorism assistance to East Africa and peacekeeping and stability efforts in Somalia.

As of November 1, 2013, State reported disbursing $42.3 million of the $104 million allocated for PREACT from fiscal years 2009 through 2013. Since 2009, State allocated PREACT assistance to countries near Somalia, as shown below.

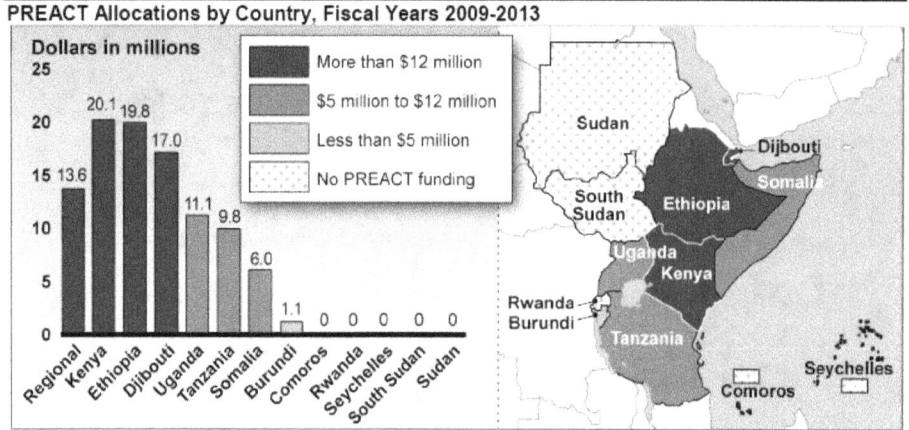

PREACT Allocations by Country, Fiscal Years 2009-2013

Source: GAO based on State Department data; Map Resources (map). | GAO-14-502

State considers key factors in managing PREACT but lacks comprehensive documentation of factors considered when selecting activities and does not routinely maintain information on the status of PREACT activities or funding. Presidential Policy Directive 23 highlights key factors—partner country needs, absorptive capacity, sustainment capacity, U.S. efforts, and other donor efforts—as critical to building partner capacity and focusing limited resources. State reported considering these key factors when selecting PREACT activities. However, State did not consistently document its consideration of the five factors. In addition, State's *Foreign Affairs Manual* calls for managers to collect program information to inform decision making and reporting. However, State does not routinely collect PREACT activity and financial information from implementing partners to enable it to have complete information needed to inform program management and accurately report on PREACT. For example, GAO discovered that State mistakenly allocated PREACT funds to Mauritius, which is not a PREACT partner, and the managing bureau was unaware of $3 million in unobligated balances in Antiterrorism Assistance that are no longer available for obligation. Routinely collecting such information, as the *Standards for Internal Control in the Federal Government* calls for, could enhance PREACT managers' ability to make operating decisions, monitor performance, and allocate resources.

_____ United States Government Accountability Office

Contents

Figures

Abbreviations

AFRICOM	U.S. Africa Command
AMISOM	African Union Mission in Somalia
ATA	Antiterrorism Assistance
DOD	U.S. Department of Defense
EARSI	East Africa Regional Strategic Initiative
ESF	Economic Support Fund
INCLE	International Narcotics Control and Law Enforcement
INL	Bureau of International Narcotics and Law Enforcement Affairs
NADR	Nonproliferation, Antiterrorism, Demining, and Related Programs
PKO	Peacekeeping Operations
PREACT	Partnership for Regional East Africa Counterterrorism
TIP	Terrorist Interdiction Program
TSCTP	Trans-Sahara Counterterrorism Partnership
USAID	U.S. Agency for International Development

GAO

U.S. GOVERNMENT ACCOUNTABILITY OFFICE

441 G St. N.W.
Washington, DC 20548

June 17, 2014

The Honorable Robert Menendez
Chairman
The Honorable Bob Corker
Ranking Member
Committee on Foreign Relations
United States Senate

In 1998, al Qaeda operatives detonated truck bombs outside two U.S. embassies in East Africa (Kenya and Tanzania). Several of the terrorists that participated in that attack found refuge in Somalia. Since then, officials report that the primary source of instability in East Africa emanates from al Shabaab, the al Qaeda-affiliated terrorist organization in Somalia. Al Shabaab conducted its first major international assault in 2010, bombing two restaurants in Kampala, Uganda, during the World Cup soccer tournament. More recently, in September 2013, al Shabaab claimed credit for attacking the Westgate Mall in Nairobi, Kenya, where nearly 200 people were injured—including Americans—and more than 60 people were killed.

To enhance its efforts to combat violent extremists, such as al Qaeda and al Shabaab, the United States launched the Partnership for Regional East Africa Counterterrorism (PREACT) in 2009 as the U.S. government initiative for counterterrorism capacity building in East Africa. PREACT is managed by the Department of State (State) to provide law enforcement, military, development, and public diplomacy assistance in 12 partner countries: Burundi, Comoros, Djibouti, Ethiopia, Kenya, Rwanda, Seychelles, Somalia, South Sudan, Sudan, Tanzania, and Uganda.[1] State has allocated a total of about $104 million for PREACT activities since 2009.

You asked us to review several issues related to PREACT. This report reviews (1) the role PREACT plays in U.S. counterterrorism assistance to

---

[1] GAO has also reviewed a similar program focused on West Africa, the Trans-Sahara Counterterrorism Partnership (TSCTP). The report is expected to be published in late June 2014. For GAO's previous report on TSCTP, see GAO, *Combating Terrorism: Actions Needed to Enhance Implementation of Trans-Sahara Counterterrorism Partnership*, GAO-08-860 (Washington, D.C.: July 31, 2008).

GAO-14-502 Combating Terrorism

East Africa, (2) the extent to which funds allocated for PREACT since 2009 have been disbursed, and (3) the extent to which PREACT decision-making processes consider key factors and other information to inform program management.

To support our work for all three objectives, we reviewed agency documents from the Departments of State, Defense, Justice, the Treasury, and Homeland Security, and the U.S. Agency for International Development (USAID). We interviewed U.S. officials from those agencies in Washington, D.C.; the U.S. Africa Command (AFRICOM) in Germany; and at U.S. missions in Djibouti, Ethiopia, and Uganda. We also met with officials from the Office of the Director of National Intelligence. To examine the role PREACT plays in U.S. counterterrorism assistance to East Africa, we reviewed national, agency, and program strategic plans; information on activities implemented; and other relevant information. To determine the extent to which funds allocated for PREACT have been disbursed, we collected data from State on funds allocated, obligated, and disbursed for PREACT activities for fiscal years 2009 through 2013. We also collected allocation data from State for other counterterrorism assistance.[2] To assess the reliability of all data provided, we reviewed information from State regarding the underlying data systems and the checks, controls, and reviews used to generate the data and ensure their accuracy and reliability. We found the data sufficiently reliable for our purposes. To determine the extent to which State uses key information to manage PREACT, we reviewed agency guidance, country assessments, activity proposals, and interagency agreements. (For further details of our objectives, scope, and methodology, see app. I.)

We conducted this performance audit from July 2013 to June 2014 in accordance with generally accepted government auditing standards. Those standards require that we plan and perform the audit to obtain sufficient, appropriate evidence to provide a reasonable basis for our findings and conclusions based on our audit objectives. We believe that the evidence obtained provides a reasonable basis for our findings and conclusions based on our audit objectives.

---

[2]For the purposes of this report, "other counterterrorism assistance" includes those activities funded by the U.S. government that support PREACT's goals, but that were not funded using PREACT-designated money. U.S. military operations, law enforcement investigations, and intelligence activities are not included.

Background

The Terrorist Threat in East Africa

The greatest terrorist threat in East Africa currently emanates from Somalia.[3] This country, which has lacked a stable government since 1991, created the environment that provided a safe haven for al Qaeda and led to the rise of al Shabaab. Between 1998 and 2012, when the latest data were available, there were 334 terrorist attacks by either al Qaeda or al Shabaab in East Africa, with the vast majority occurring in Somalia, as illustrated in figure 1. The United States designated al Qaeda as a Foreign Terrorist Organization in October 1999 and designated al Shabaab as a Foreign Terrorist Organization in March 2008.[4] Other violent organizations, such as the Lord's Resistance Army, are also active in East Africa but have not been designated as Foreign Terrorist Organizations by State.[5]

---

[3]GAO reported on U.S. assistance to Somalia in 2008. See GAO, *Somalia: Several Challenges Limit U.S. and International Stabilization, Humanitarian, and Development Efforts*, GAO-08-351 (Washington, D.C.: Feb. 19, 2008).

[4]To be designated a Foreign Terrorist Organization by State, an organization must meet the following criteria: (1) be a foreign organization; (2) engage in terrorist activity or terrorism (as defined by U.S. law) or retain the capability and intent to engage in terrorist activity or terrorism; and (3) the organization's terrorist activity or terrorism must threaten the security of U.S. nationals or the national security (national defense, foreign relations, or the economic interests) of the United States. 8 U.S.C. § 1189.

[5]Although the Lord's Resistance Army has not been designated as a Foreign Terrorist Organization, this group has been designated on State's Terrorist Exclusion List, a separate designation for immigration purposes. See 8 U.S.C. § 1182 for Terrorist Exclusion List designation authority.

Figure 1: Reported Terrorist Attacks by al Qaeda and al Shabaab in Partnership for Regional East Africa Counterterrorism (PREACT) Countries, 1998-2012

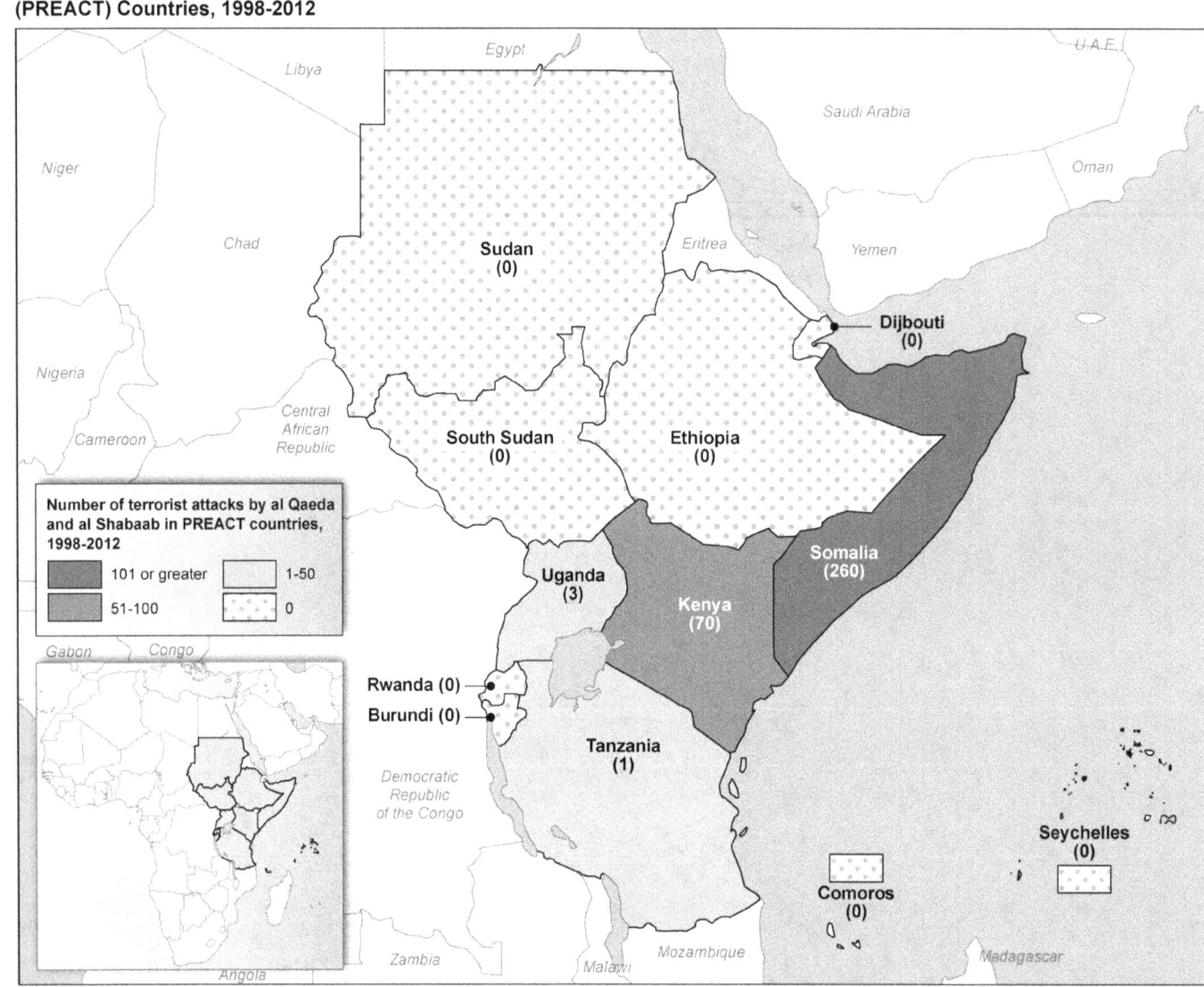

Source: GAO analysis of the National Consortium for the Study of Terrorism and Responses to Terrorism's Global Terrorism Database, and Map Resources (map). | GAO-14-502

Notes: Terrorist events conducted by al Qaeda and al Shabaab are included in the graphic. This graphic only includes events that the National Consortium for the Study of Terrorism and Responses to Terrorism identified as events (1) aimed at attaining a political, economic, religious, or social goal; (2) occurring where there was evidence of an intention to coerce, intimidate, or convey a message beyond the immediate victims; (3) falling outside legitimate warfare activities and the parameters of international humanitarian law; and, (4) that are not ambiguous as to their nature as terrorist incidents. Successful and unsuccessful attacks are included. Terrorist event information is drawn entirely from publicly available materials and reflects what is reported in those sources. (National Consortium for the Study of Terrorism and Responses to Terrorism). (2012). Global Terrorism Database, Incidents Over Time. Retrieved from http://www.start.umd.edu/gtd on May 6, 2014.)

According to many experts, the unstable situation in Somalia is a particularly important factor fueling the spread of violent radicalism in eastern Africa today and poses a great risk to U.S. national security. We reported in June 2011 that Somalia ranked third, behind Yemen and Pakistan, as one of the countries that pose the greatest risk to U.S. national security.[6] In 1991, armed opposition groups overthrew the existing Somali government, resulting in turmoil, factional fighting, and anarchy. Until recently, Somalia lacked a functioning central government. This tumultuous environment provided a safe haven for al Qaeda after the 1998 attacks and led to the rise of al Shabaab. Since then, there have been at least 15 attempts to establish a federal government. Somalia had operated without a permanent national government or a national legal system from 1991 through 2012. However, recent gains in stability led the United States to formally recognize the government of Somalia in January 2013.

Al Qaeda's involvement in East Africa goes back more than 20 years. In 1989, a militant government seized power in Sudan and established contact with al Qaeda leadership, who subsequently moved people and financial assets into the country. In the early 1990s, al Qaeda began building cells in other East African nations, such as Kenya and Somalia. In 1998, it conducted simultaneous terrorist attacks against the U.S. embassies in Kenya and Tanzania. Al Qaeda has claimed responsibility for other attacks in East Africa, including the 2002 coordinated attacks in Mombassa, Kenya; Al Qaeda bombed a hotel—killing 15 people and injuring another 35—and unsuccessfully fired missiles at a passenger airplane departing from the airport. Some experts argue that al Qaeda has decreased its direct operations in East Africa and instead provides ideological direction to other militant groups located in the region.

Al Shabaab is an al Qaeda affiliate.[7] It began as the militant wing of the former Somali Islamic Courts Union that took control of most of southern

---

[6]See GAO, *Combating Terrorism: U.S. Government Should Improve Its Reporting on Terrorist Safe Havens*, GAO-11-561 (Washington, D.C.: June 3, 2011). GAO spoke with 13 subject matter experts with knowledge related to terrorist safe havens and asked them to determine which five terrorist safe havens identified in State's August 2010 Country Reports on Terrorism posed the greatest risk to U.S. national security.

[7]Al Shabaab declared its ties to al Qaeda in February 2012.

Somalia in 2006.[8] Since then, al Shabaab has led an insurgency against the transitional government and international peacekeepers in Somalia. At various times, the group has controlled strategic locations in southern and central Somalia. Al Shabaab has claimed responsibility for bombings and shootings throughout Somalia as well as assassinations of government officials, journalists, and peace activists. The group also claimed responsibility for the July 2010 suicide bomb attacks in Kampala, Uganda, which killed more than 70 people. More recently, it claimed responsibility for the attack on the Westgate Mall in Nairobi, Kenya, which killed more than 60 people.

U.S. Approach to Terrorism in East Africa

The *U.S. National Strategy for Counterterrorism* (the National Strategy), approved in 2011, articulates the government's approach to countering terrorism and focuses on disrupting, degrading, dismantling, and defeating al Qaeda and its affiliates.[9] The National Strategy lists East Africa as one of nine global priority regions.[10] The National Strategy's section on East Africa states that the goal for that region is to dismantle al Qaeda elements—including elements embedded within al Shabaab— while building the capacity of countries and local administrations to counter the terrorist threat. To achieve these goals, the United States uses an array of tools implemented by several agencies, including those that require direct action by the United States. For example, Department of Defense (DOD) officials stated that they have the authority through a presidential order to conduct direct military operations that can be specific to designated members of al Qaeda and its affiliates. The Department of the Treasury (Treasury) addresses money laundering and terrorist

[8]State reports that al Shabaab has roots in the al-Ittihad al-Islami terrorist organization, which rose to prominence in the Horn of Africa in the early 1990s.

[9]The National Strategy's eight overarching goals are to (1) protect the American people, homeland, and American interests; (2) disrupt, degrade, dismantle, and defeat al Qaeda and its affiliates and adherents; (3) prevent terrorist development, acquisition, and use of weapons of mass destruction; (4) eliminate safe havens; (5) build enduring counterterrorism partnerships and capabilities; (6) degrade links between al Qaeda and its affiliates and adherents; (7) counter al Qaeda ideology and its resonance and diminish the specific drivers of violence that al Qaeda exploits; and, (8) deprive terrorists of their enabling means.

[10]The National Strategy's nine priority regions are (in order): the homeland, South Asia, Arabian Peninsula, East Africa, Europe, Iraq, the Maghreb and Sahel, South-East Asia, and Central Asia. The National Strategy also has one other area of focus that is not geographical: information and ideas (al Qaeda ideology, messaging, and resonance).

financing threats, and administers and enforces counterterrorism sanctions.[11] The Department of Justice investigates and prosecutes terrorists. The National Strategy also emphasizes the need to build foreign partnerships and capacity and to strengthen U.S. resilience. Many U.S. agencies also have programs that work with partner nations to increase the capacity of their military, legal, and financial systems.

The United States also partners with other countries and multilateral institutions to achieve its counterterrorism goals. In particular, the United States has supported the African Union Mission in Somalia (AMISOM), a peacekeeping mission first authorized by the United Nations Security Council in 2007. AMISOM has a military component staffed with troops from Uganda, Burundi, Djibouti, Kenya, Ethiopia, and Sierra Leone.[12]

PREACT was designed to be the U.S. government initiative for long-term engagement and capacity building to combat evolving terrorist threats in East Africa.[13] State created a guiding strategy for PREACT in 2009, which it updated in 2013 in consultation with the Departments of Defense, Justice, Homeland Security, and the Treasury, and with USAID.[14] The PREACT program is managed by State's regional Bureau of African Affairs, but draws on the expertise of several other bureaus and U.S. agencies to implement its activities, as depicted in figure 2.

---

[11]According to Treasury Officials, the functions of the Office of Terrorism and Financial Intelligence include providing policy, strategic, and operational direction to the Treasury on issues relating to: terrorist financing; financial crimes, including money laundering, counterfeiting and other offenses threatening the integrity of the financial system; United States economic sanctions programs; implementation of the Bank Secrecy Act, as amended, other enforcement matters; certain intelligence analysis and coordination functions; and certain security functions and programs of the Treasury.

[12]Uganda, Burundi, Djibouti, Kenya, and Ethiopia are PREACT countries. Sierra Leone is not.

[13]PREACT was formerly known as the East Africa Regional Strategic Initiative.

[14]State also reported that it has established an annual strategic planning process involving U.S. embassies to validate PREACT's priorities and evaluate its overall progress.

Figure 2: Organization of the Partnership for Regional East Africa Counterterrorism (PREACT)

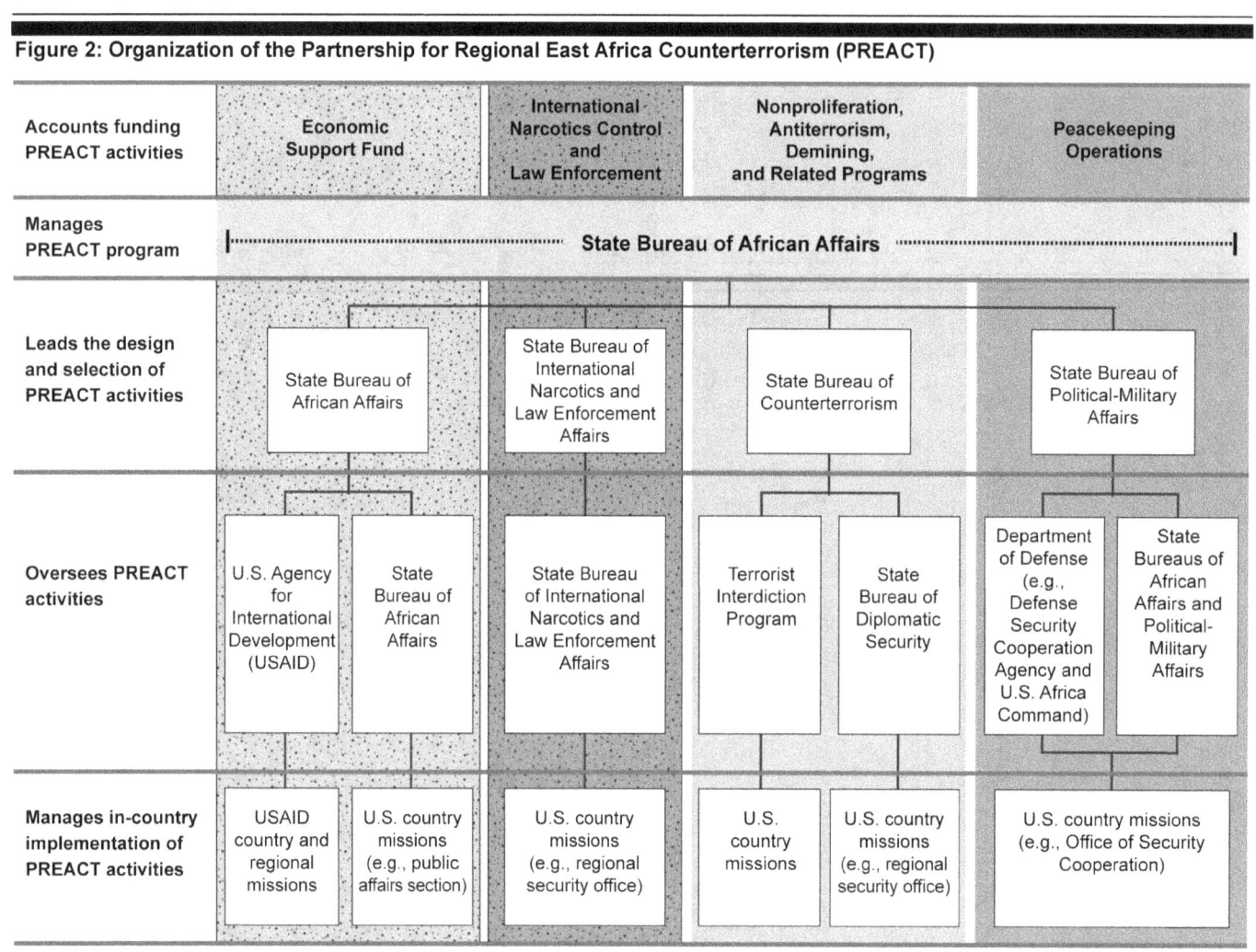

Accounts funding PREACT activities	Economic Support Fund		International Narcotics Control and Law Enforcement	Nonproliferation, Antiterrorism, Demining, and Related Programs		Peacekeeping Operations	
Manages PREACT program	State Bureau of African Affairs						
Leads the design and selection of PREACT activities	State Bureau of African Affairs		State Bureau of International Narcotics and Law Enforcement Affairs	State Bureau of Counterterrorism		State Bureau of Political-Military Affairs	
Oversees PREACT activities	U.S. Agency for International Development (USAID)	State Bureau of African Affairs	State Bureau of International Narcotics and Law Enforcement Affairs	Terrorist Interdiction Program	State Bureau of Diplomatic Security	Department of Defense (e.g., Defense Security Cooperation Agency and U.S. Africa Command)	State Bureaus of African Affairs and Political-Military Affairs
Manages in-country implementation of PREACT activities	USAID country and regional missions	U.S. country missions (e.g., public affairs section)	U.S. country missions (e.g., regional security office)	U.S. country missions	U.S. country missions (e.g., regional security office)	U.S. country missions (e.g., Office of Security Cooperation)	

PREACT   U.S. Partnership for Regional East Africa Counterterrorism

Source: GAO analysis of State Department information. | GAO-14-502

Note: In addition to the agencies listed above, State has involved other U.S. government agencies in creating PREACT's strategy, such as the Departments of Justice, the Treasury, and Homeland Security. While these agencies could partner with State to implement PREACT activities, they have not received any PREACT funding to date.

PREACT activities are funded by four State-managed U.S. foreign assistance accounts:

- Economic Support Fund (ESF) authorizes the President to assist various countries and organizations in order to promote economic or political stability, and has also been specifically appropriated for programs to counter extremism in East Africa.

- International Narcotics Control and Law Enforcement (INCLE) authorizes the President to assist foreign countries and international organizations in controlling narcotics and other controlled substances, or for other anticrime purposes. For example, INCLE funds have been used to develop and implement policies and programs that maintain the rule of law and strengthen institutional law enforcement and judicial capabilities, including combating transnational crime.

- Nonproliferation, Antiterrorism, Demining, and Related Programs (NADR) authorizes the President to provide antiterrorism assistance, nonproliferation and export control assistance, and other assistance to foreign countries for various purposes. PREACT is funded specifically through two NADR programs: Antiterrorism Assistance (ATA), which is used to furnish assistance to foreign countries in order to enhance the ability of their law enforcement personnel to deter, detect, and respond to terrorist attacks, and the Terrorist Interdiction Program (TIP), which assists in building immigration capacity in foreign countries to identify the attempted travel of known or suspected terrorists.

- Peacekeeping Operations (PKO) authorizes the President to furnish assistance to friendly countries and international organizations for peacekeeping operations and other programs carried out in furtherance of the national security interests of the United States. PKO funds are used, in part, to train and equip military units tasked with monitoring and controlling border areas and territory exploited by terrorist elements.

PREACT Supports Broader U.S. Government Counterterrorism Efforts in East Africa

PREACT is a regional program that serves as one part of the overall U.S. counterterrorism assistance to East Africa, providing counterterrorism capacity-building assistance to 12 East African countries. Officials from State and other U.S. agencies view PREACT as a valuable component of U.S. counterterrorism assistance in East Africa.

PREACT Is a Regional Program That Provides Capacity Building Assistance to Partner Nations

PREACT's five goals focus on improving partner nations' military counterterrorism capacity, rule-of-law framework, border security, ability to counter violent extremism, and ability to counter terrorist financing. State has funded activities to support four of PREACT's five goals; PREACT funds have not been used to counter terrorist financing. The following are examples of activities implemented to help achieve PREACT goals:[15]

- *Improve the institutional and operational capacity of militaries to participate in regional counterterrorism operations.* To achieve this goal, State's Bureau of African Affairs generally implements activities through DOD's AFRICOM, using PKO funding. For example, AFRICOM has implemented or planned activities such as providing the Navy of Djibouti with small boats to assist with counterterrorism and force protection; providing intermediate-level aviation maintenance training and spare parts for the Kenya Army fleet of helicopters, and organizing a regional best practices forum regarding military logistics for several PREACT countries. In one case, however, State directly funded a contractor to implement an activity. Specifically, State provided the Ethiopian military with communications equipment, training, and a dedicated communications adviser. Figure 3 illustrates a few PREACT activities aimed at improving the counterterrorism capabilities of partner countries' militaries.

---

[15]Activities identified are meant to serve as examples of PREACT-funded U.S. counterterrorism capacity-building efforts, not to provide an exhaustive list of all U.S. activities to address counterterrorism capacity building in East Africa.

Figure 3: Illustrations of Partnership for Regional East Africa Counterterrorism (PREACT) Activities Supporting Military Capacity Building in Partner Countries

Kenya maintenance training

Regional training held in Tanzania

Ethiopia communications equipment and training

Djiboutian Navy boat provided by PREACT

Source: Department of State. | GAO-14-502

- *Develop a rule-of-law framework for countering terrorism and building law enforcement and justice sector capacity.* To achieve the goal of detecting, disrupting, and prosecuting terrorist activities, State's

Bureau of African Affairs generally implements activities through other State bureaus such as International Narcotics and Law Enforcement Affairs (INL), which manages the INCLE account, or Diplomatic Security's Office of Antiterrorism Assistance, which implements activities using the NADR/ATA funding account. According to State officials, INL activities focus on the institutional reform and foundational skill sets of the criminal justice sector, while ATA activities focus on specialized counterterrorism law enforcement training. INL has implemented projects such as enhancing a police forensics laboratory to help the Tanzanian Police Force fight and deter crime, including terrorism. The Office of Antiterrorism Assistance has provided numerous trainings on topics such as investigating terrorist incidents in Djibouti and Somalia, fraudulent documents recognition in Burundi, and cyber forensics in Tanzania, as shown in figure 4.

Figure 4: Antiterrorism Cyber Forensics Training in Tanzania

Source: Department of State. | GAO-14-502

- *Enhance border security to restrain terrorist movement.* To achieve this goal, State's Bureau of African Affairs generally implements activities through DOD's AFRICOM and through State's Bureaus of

Counterterrorism and Diplomatic Security. AFRICOM has equipped and trained a technical platoon in Kenya that supports counterterrorism and border security operations in the northern part of Kenya. In addition, the Bureau of Counterterrorism manages TIP, which provides partner countries with training and equipment for screening at 38 port-of-entry locations in five PREACT countries.[16] State's Bureau of Diplomatic Security has also implemented trainings on border security (see fig. 5).

Figure 5: Antiterrorism Maritime Border Security Training in Tanzania

Source: Department of State. | GAO-14-502

- *Reduce the appeal of violent extremism.* To achieve this goal, State's Bureau of African Affairs generally implements activities using ESF assistance by partnering with USAID or public affairs sections at U.S. missions. USAID has used funds designated for PREACT programs in both Kenya and Somalia to counter al Shabaab's efforts to reach disenfranchised youth and to promote democratic governance and political participation by using social media, radio, theater, and music; rehabilitating community centers; and supporting local groups. As shown in figure 6, State has directly funded projects such as computer training to teachers working with at-risk youth in Kenya and Uganda.

---

[16] In 2011, GAO reported on TIP and other U.S. government efforts to build partner countries' capacity to prevent terrorist travel. See GAO, *Combating Terrorism: Additional Steps Needed to Enhance Foreign Partners' Capacity to Prevent Terrorist Travel,* GAO-11-637 (Washington, D.C.: June 30, 2011).

Figure 6: Examples of Partnership for Regional East Africa Counterterrorism (PREACT) Activities Aimed at Reducing the Appeal of Violent Extremism in Partner Countries

Kenya computer skills training

Uganda computer training for youth and community leaders

Source: Department of State. | GAO-14-502

- *Countering the financing of terrorism.* State's Bureau of African Affairs has not used funds designated for PREACT to achieve this goal, in part because, according to State officials, the financial systems in many of the partner nations are currently not sophisticated enough to absorb such specialized assistance. However, using non-PREACT funds from the NADR account, State does support activities to enhance some PREACT countries' ability to investigate financial crimes. For example, State funds Treasury's efforts to help Kenya and Tanzania improve their Financial Intelligence Units.

U.S. Officials View PREACT as a Valuable Part of Overall U.S. Counterterrorism Assistance to East Africa

PREACT is one part of overall U.S. efforts to combat terrorism in East Africa, and officials report that it is a valuable complement to other counterterrorism activities. From 2009 through 2013, PREACT has accounted for about 11 percent (about $104 million) of overall U.S. assistance to combat terrorism in East Africa (about $967 million). In addition to PREACT, the United States has provided about $348 million in other U.S. counterterrorism assistance for East Africa, including activities funded by, for example, State's bilateral counterterrorism capacity-building efforts, DOD's global security sector assistance programs, or USAID's programs to counter violent extremism.[17] In addition, since fiscal year 2009, State has provided about $516 million to fund efforts in Somalia, as shown in figure 7.[18] U.S. assistance to Somalia has provided, in part, training and equipment for troops deploying to AMISOM and to support logistics, training, equipment, and other support to the Somalia National Security Forces. While this assistance is not explicitly labeled as counterterrorism assistance, officials reported that U.S. efforts to stabilize Somalia support PREACT's counterterrorism goals because Somalia is the safe haven for al Shabaab.

---

[17]For the purposes of this report, "other counterterrorism assistance" includes those activities funded by the U.S. government that support PREACT's goals, but that were not funded using PREACT-designated money. U.S. military operations, law enforcement investigations, and intelligence activities are not included.

[18]The amount provided to Somalia does not include the United States' assessed contributions to the United Nations' Support Office for AMISOM.

Figure 7: Funds Allocated for U.S. Assistance to Combat Terrorism in East Africa, Fiscal Years 2009-2013

Total $967.5 (Dollars in millions)

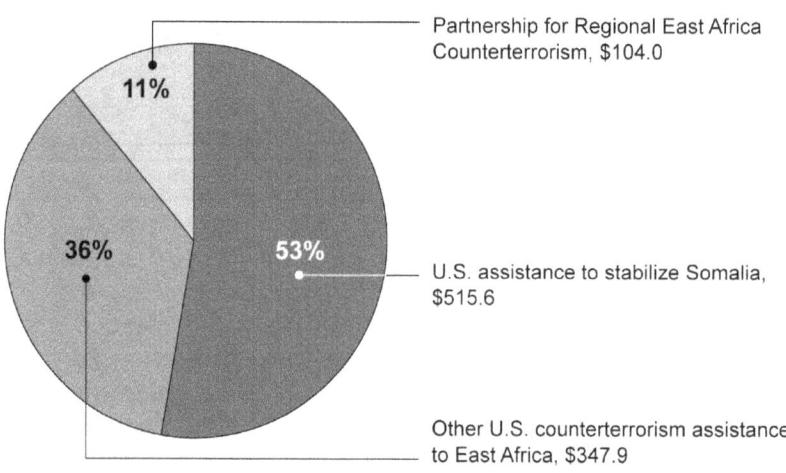

Partnership for Regional East Africa Counterterrorism, $104.0

U.S. assistance to stabilize Somalia, $515.6

Other U.S. counterterrorism assistance to East Africa, $347.9

Source: GAO analysis of State Department data. | GAO-14-502

Officials from State and DOD report that PREACT funding is a valuable complement to other counterterrorism assistance for several reasons:

- *Funds for PREACT programs are dedicated to counterterrorism assistance in East Africa, whereas other counterterrorism assistance may be used more broadly around the globe.* Officials from AFRICOM stated that the targeted nature of PREACT funds helps them plan their programming in East Africa. For example, they can anticipate receiving about $10 million annually for East Africa from the PKO account for PREACT, whereas the availability of funds from other sources may vary widely from year to year depending on shifting global priorities.

- *PREACT provides multi-year funds, which give implementing entities more time to plan and implement a program.* The accounts funding PREACT programs, except for PKO, are generally available for obligation for more than 1 fiscal year in appropriations laws. For example, appropriations for NADR, ESF, and INCLE are generally available for obligation for 2 fiscal years, giving implementing entities more time to plan and implement a program. Officials from AFRICOM reported that the flexible nature of PKO funds they receive through PREACT allows them to better implement an activity.[19] Officials report that DOD's process for assigning military personnel and troops can be lengthy and that sometimes DOD cannot get its units into place fast enough to carry out a project within the 1-year timeframe required by some other programs. PREACT-designated funds allow them more flexibility.

- *As financing for a regional program, PREACT funds do not need to be allocated for a specific country in advance and can be reprogrammed from one PREACT country to another to address implementation challenges or emerging needs.* For example, State planned to fund a Resident Legal Advisor position in Burundi using PREACT funds. However, State had difficulty coming to an agreement with the Burundian government on the exact parameters of the program and could not get the program started. PREACT was able to reprogram that money to be used to fund a Resident Legal Advisor position in Uganda. Officials reported that, had the money for the position been programmed bilaterally to Burundi, it would have taken longer to shift it from one country to another.

- *The nature of PREACT also encourages implementing entities to view counterterrorism from a regional perspective, rather than country by country.* For example, officials from State's Bureau of Counterterrorism report that TIP has focused its resources on countries surrounding Somalia to address East Africa's primary terrorist threat, al Shabaab. Officials from DOD report that PREACT allows them to provide regional training in a centralized location or similar training, maintenance, and equipment to several countries bilaterally. With PREACT money, AFRICOM has been able to introduce a standardized set of 10 courses focused on developing intelligence corps in several PREACT countries to better enable the countries to share intelligence.

---

[19]The funds officials referred to were PKO funds, which are generally available for obligation for 1 year. However, under certain authority generally granted in the State, Foreign Operations, and Related Appropriations acts, if these funds are obligated within the period of availability, they may be deobligated and remain available for obligation for an additional 4 years. These funds remain available for expenditure for an additional 5 years after the period of availability for obligation. See, e.g., Pub. L. No. 113-76, § 7011, Jan. 17, 2014.

State Has Disbursed $42.3 Million of the Nearly $104 Million Allocated for PREACT

For fiscal years 2009 through 2013, State allocated about $104 million for PREACT, of which it had disbursed $42.3 million by November 2013. State allocated funds for PREACT activities from four foreign assistance accounts to 7 of the 12 PREACT countries.[20]

State Allocated About $104 Million for PREACT from Fiscal Years 2009 through 2013

For fiscal years 2009 through 2013, State allocated nearly $104 million for PREACT from four foreign assistance accounts: ESF, INCLE, NADR, and PKO.[21] As shown in figure 8, State allocated the majority of resources for PREACT from PKO (about $45 million) and NADR (about $45 million), and allocated about $8 million from ESF and $6 million from INCLE.

---

[20]At the time of reporting, the most recent data available on funding for PREACT were as of November 2013.

[21]In the Consolidated Appropriations Act, 2010, Congress mandated that not less than $24,735,000 shall be made available from certain accounts for the East Africa Regional Strategic Initiative (EARSI), the predecessor of PREACT. However, State allocated only $24,628,000 for EARSI/PREACT from this appropriation (Pub. L. No. 111-117, § 7070(b)(1), Dec. 16, 2009). In the Consolidated Appropriations Act, 2012, Congress mandated that not less than $21,300,000 from that appropriation should be made available for PREACT, and State allocated $23,322,000 for PREACT from this appropriation (Pub. L. No. 112-74, § 7043(b), Dec. 23, 2011).

Figure 8: Percentages of U.S. Funds Allocated for Partnership for Regional East Africa Counterterrorism (PREACT), Fiscal Years 2009-2013, as of November 2013

Total $104.0 (Dollars in millions)

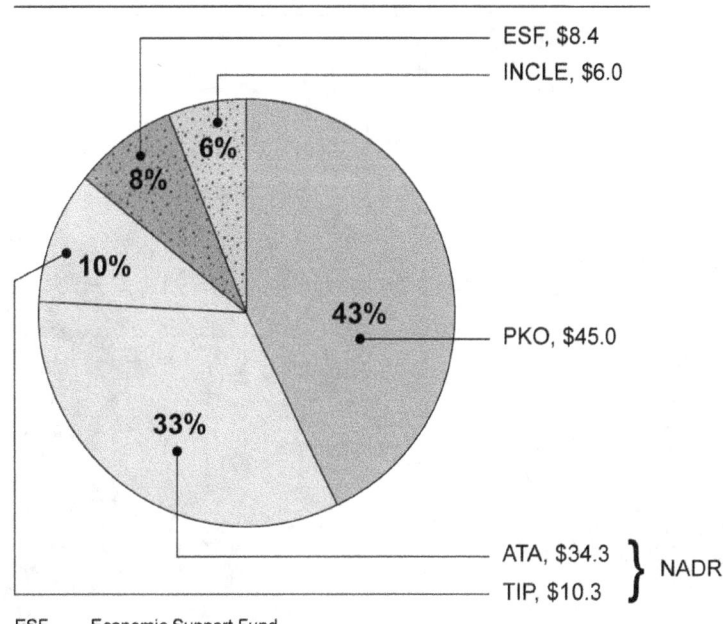

ESF	Economic Support Fund
INCLE	International Narcotics Control and Law Enforcement
NADR	Nonproliferation, Antiterrorism, Demining, and Related Programs
	ATA Antiterrorism Assistance
	TIP Terrorist Interdiction Program
PKO	Peacekeeping Operations

Source: GAO analysis of State Department data. | GAO-14-502

State allocated funds for PREACT activities for 7 of the 12 PREACT partner countries. The largest amounts of funds for PREACT activities were allocated for Kenya, Ethiopia, and Djibouti, which border Somalia (see fig. 9). In addition, 13 percent of funding for PREACT activities was allocated for regional activities that benefited multiple PREACT countries.

Figure 9: U.S. Funds Allocated for Partnership for Regional East Africa Counterterrorism (PREACT), by Country, Fiscal Years 2009-2013, as of November 2013

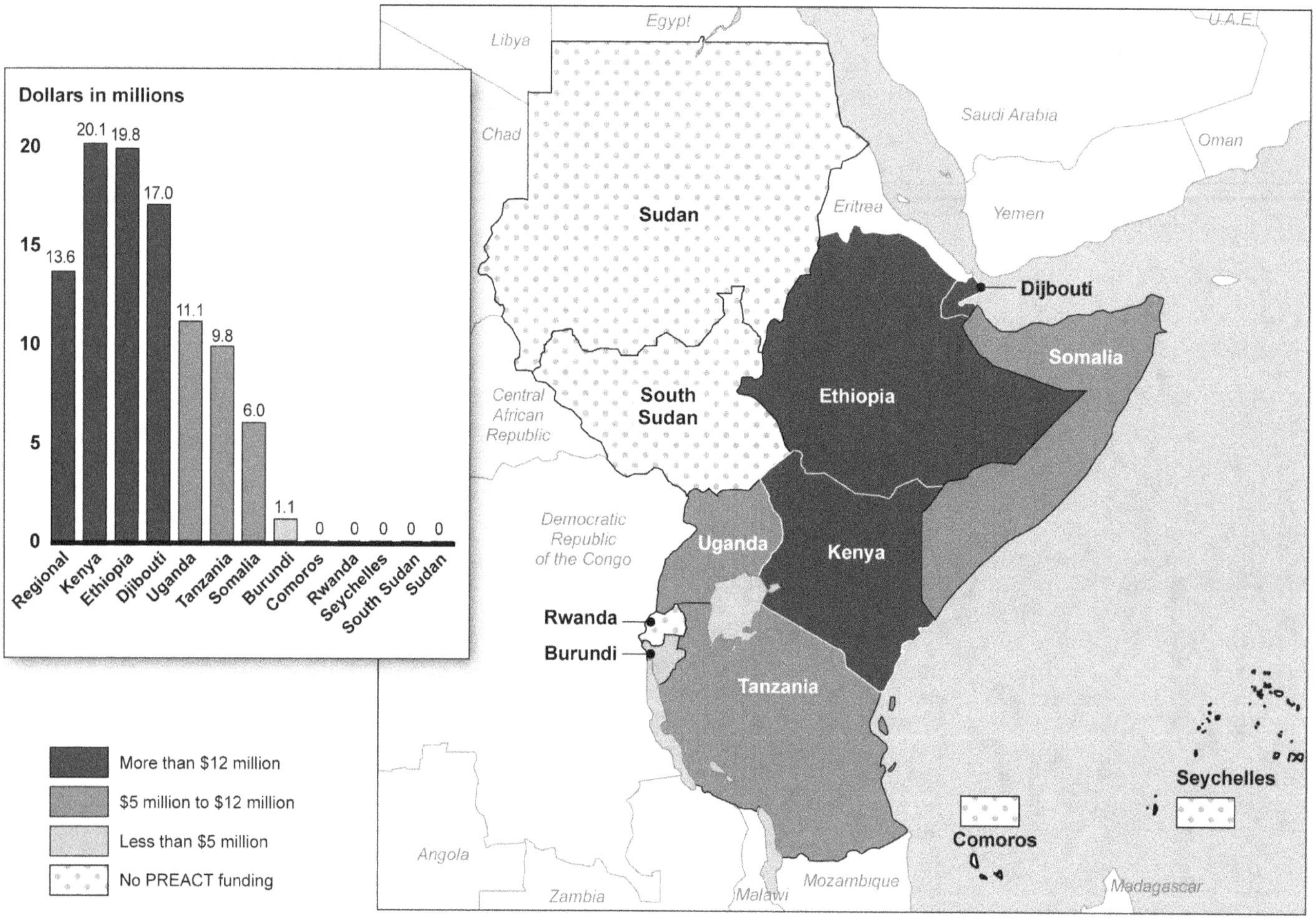

Source: GAO based on State Department data; Map Resources (map). | GAO-14-502

Note: State also allocated approximately $1 million of the funds for PREACT for program management for fiscal years 2009 through 2013. In addition, State allocated $300,000 of funds for PREACT for Mauritius, which is not a PREACT partner.

State Has Disbursed $42.3 Million in PREACT Funding from Fiscal Years 2009 through 2013

As of November 2013, State reported disbursing $42.3 million of the nearly $104 million allocated for PREACT from fiscal years 2009 through 2013, as shown in table 1. An additional $45 million has been obligated for PREACT activities but not disbursed. As of November 2013, State had an unobligated balance of $16.7 million. The majority (81 percent, or $13.6 million) of the unobligated balance was appropriated in fiscal year

GAO-14-502 Combating Terrorism

2013 and remains available for obligation, and State is in the process of obligating these funds. The remaining unobligated balance of $3.1 million is from NADR/ATA funds appropriated in fiscal years 2009 through 2012, and according to State officials, the period of availability to incur new obligations has expired. These unobligated balances remain available for an additional 5 fiscal years for recording and adjusting obligations properly chargeable to the appropriations period of availability. For example, these funds may remain available for contract modifications properly within the scope of the original contract.

Table 1: Status of U.S. Funds Allocated for Partnership for Regional East Africa Counterterrorism (PREACT) Activities, Fiscal Years 2009-2013, as of November 2013

Dollars in thousands

	2009	2010	2011	2012	2013	Total
Allocated	11,481	24,648	20,947	23,322	23,598	**103,995**
Unobligated balance	829[a]	881[a]	532[a]	871[a]	13,598[b]	**16,711**
Unliquidated obligations	2,891	8,813	9,136	14,174	9,986	**45,000**
Disbursed	7,761	14,954	11,280	8,277	14	**42,286**

Source: GAO analysis of State Department data. | GAO-14-502

Notes: The amounts above reflect totals from ESF, INCLE, PKO, and NADR funds dedicated for PREACT activities appropriated by fiscal year. For the status of each account's unobligated balance by fiscal year, see app. II.

[a]This unobligated balance is from NADR/ATA and, according to State officials, the period of availability to incur new obligations has expired. These unobligated balances remain available for an additional 5 fiscal years for recording and adjusting obligations properly chargeable to the appropriation's period of availability. For example, these funds may remain available for contract modifications properly within the scope of the original contract.

[b]This unobligated balance is from ESF, INCLE, NADR/ATA, and NADR/TIP and reflects fiscal year 2013 appropriations that remain available for obligation and State is in the process of obligating these funds.

As shown in table 2, NADR (both ATA and TIP) accounted for the majority of funds disbursed between fiscal years 2009 and 2013 for PREACT. (See app. II for greater detail on the status of U.S. funds allocated for PREACT, by account and fiscal year.)

Table 2: Status of U.S. Funds Allocated for Partnership for Regional East Africa Counterterrorism (PREACT) Activities by Account, Fiscal Years 2009-2013, as of November 2013

Dollars in thousands

Account	Allocated	Unobligated balance	Unliquidated obligations	Disbursed
ESF	8,439	1,900[a]	1,777	4,762
INCLE	6,000	2,000[a]	3,318	682
NADR/ATA	34,316	11,650[b]	2,917	19,750
NADR/TIP	10,281	1,161[a]	0	9,120
PKO	44,960	0	36,988	7,972
PREACT Total	**103,995**	**16,711**	**45,000**	**42,286**

ESF	Economic Support Fund
INCLE	International Narcotics Control and Law Enforcement
NADR	Nonproliferation, Antiterrorism, Demining, and Related Programs
ATA	Antiterrorism Assistance
TIP	Terrorist Interdiction Program
PKO	Peacekeeping Operations

Source: GAO analysis of State Department data. | GAO-14-502

[a]Unobligated balances for ESF, INCLE, and NADR/TIP reflect fiscal year 2013 appropriations that are still available for obligation and that State is in the process of obligating these funds.

[b]The majority (73 percent, or $8.5 million) of the unobligated balance for NADR/ATA is from fiscal year 2013 appropriations that are still available for obligation and that State is in the process of obligating. The remaining unobligated balance of $3.1 million is from NADR/ATA and, according to State officials, the period of availability to incur new obligations has expired. These unobligated balances remain available for an additional 5 fiscal years for recording and adjusting obligations properly chargeable to the appropriation's period of availability. For example, these funds may remain available for contract modifications properly within the scope of the original contract.

State Considers Key Factors in Managing PREACT Initiative, but Lacks Comprehensive Documentation and Information Collection Efforts

State's Bureau of African Affairs considers key factors and information to manage PREACT using separate processes for each funding stream. However, weaknesses exist in the bureau's and State's documentation of critical factors considered when selecting activities and State's collection of PREACT activities and financial information. The presidential policy directive on security sector assistance asserts that U.S. agencies should consider several key factors when implementing security sector assistance, including partner country needs, absorptive capacity, sustainment capacity, other U.S. efforts, and other donor efforts.[22] State officials said that they consider those factors when selecting PREACT activities; however, we found that State did not consistently document its consideration. Moreover, while the Bureau of African Affairs undertakes several efforts to manage PREACT, it does not routinely collect comprehensive, PREACT-specific activity and financial information, which would be consistent with internal controls and State's *Foreign Affairs Manual*.[23] Effective internal control activities help program managers cope with shifting environments and evolving demands through effective stewardship of public resources.[24]

State Selects PREACT Activities Using Different Processes for Each Funding Stream

Since PREACT derives its funding from different foreign assistance accounts that have different authorities and broader goals beyond PREACT, State's Bureau of African Affairs, in coordination with other State bureaus, uses a separate process for each account when determining, designing, and selecting the types of PREACT activities to fund.

- *ESF*: The Bureau of African Affairs selects PREACT activities funded from ESF in coordination with the Bureau of Counterterrorism and USAID. The Bureau of African Affairs uses a proposal template to solicit proposals from U.S. missions in East Africa. Although a USAID official stressed the importance of the interagency review of

---

[22]The White House, *Presidential Policy Directive 23 on Security Sector Assistance* (Washington, D.C.: April 5, 2013).

[23]State, *Foreign Affairs Manual*, 2 FAM 022.12, 4 FAM 013 a.1, and 4 FAM 013 b.9; and also GAO, *Standards for Internal Control in the Federal Government*, GAO/AIMD-00-21.3.1, (Washington, D.C.: November, 1999), 19.

[24]According to the *Foreign Affairs Manual* and the *Standards for Internal Control in the Federal Government*, "management control" and "internal control" are synonymous.

proposals, a State official noted that bureau officials make the final decision on which PREACT activities to fund through the ESF account.

- *PKO*: The Bureau of African Affairs, along with State's Bureau of Political-Military Affairs and DOD's AFRICOM, uses a proposal process to select programs to implement activities with PKO funds. AFRICOM requests and collects proposals for counterterrorism assistance from its components and units at U.S. missions. State and DOD officials review the proposals and determine which activities will be funded through different funding streams. State officials make the final decision on which PREACT activities to fund through the PKO account.

- *INCLE*: INL determines which PREACT partner countries receive INCLE funds through PREACT, in consultation with the Bureaus of African Affairs and Counterterrorism, according to State officials. INL officials said they generally focus on partner countries that have an existing INL program.[25] According to INL officials, INL works with country mission teams to identify and develop PREACT activities. INL typically conducts in-country visits to identify needs and gaps that an INL program could address.

- *NADR*: The Bureau of African Affairs works with the Bureau of Counterterrorism to determine which countries will receive NADR assistance through ATA and TIP.

  - *ATA*: The Bureau of Counterterrorism provides policy guidance and sets programming priorities for ATA for each partner country in consultation with the Bureau of African Affairs. The Bureau of Diplomatic Security leads in-country assessments to measure law enforcement technical capabilities in the partner country and to follow up on previous training and equipment investments. According to State officials, on the basis of resources allocated for each country by the Bureaus of Counterterrorism and African Affairs, Diplomatic Security's Office of Antiterrorism Assistance either selects ATA training from a set of developed training activities or develops tailored consultations to address the capability gaps identified in the assessment.

---

[25]INL has programmed PREACT activities in Burundi, Somalia, Tanzania, and Uganda.

- *TIP*: The Bureau of Counterterrorism determines if a country meets certain prerequisites and will work with the Bureau of African Affairs to allocate TIP resources designated for PREACT to those partner countries. TIP officials look for three factors when selecting a partner country: (1) evidence of terrorist activity, (2) the need for a screening system, and (3) a willingness to work with the United States.

State Reported Considering Key Factors, but Documentation Was Inconsistent

The presidential policy directive on security sector assistance states that U.S. agencies should target security sector assistance where it can be effective.[26] To accomplish this, the directive calls for assessments that (1) identify partner country needs, (2) highlight absorptive capacity, (3) highlight sustainment capacity as necessary to sustain U.S. investments, (4) note the importance of unity of effort across the U.S. government, and (5) consider coordination with other donors. State uses different mechanisms to collect information on those five key factors.[27] In addition, the *Standards for Internal Controls in the Federal Government* states internal control activities aimed at ensuring effective use of resources should be clearly documented.[28]

State officials engaged in managing the various PREACT funding accounts reported considering the key factors of country needs, absorptive capacity, sustainment capacity, other U.S. efforts, and other donor efforts for all the funding accounts. U.S. officials provided various examples of how State considered the key factors. For example, State and DOD officials reported that officials at U.S. missions and AFRICOM components identify partner country needs by talking with partner country officials. INL officials said that during in-country visits, INL personnel gather information about the partner country's absorptive capacity. According to TIP officials, they require partner countries to sustain information technology systems. U.S. officials in Ethiopia told us that they

---

[26]Presidential Policy Directive 23 was signed by the President on April 5, 2013.

[27]According to Presidential Policy Directive 23, security sector assistance includes areas related to PREACT, such as counterterrorism, law enforcement, border security, financial crimes, rule of law, and responding to violent extremism, among other areas.

[28]*Standards for Internal Control in the Federal Government* states that internal control activities, which help government program managers achieve desired results through effective stewardship of public resources (p. 4), need to be clearly documented, and the documentation should be readily available for examination (p. 15). GAO/AIMD-00-21.3.1.

have a Security Sector Working Group that monitors all security-related assistance to coordinate U.S. efforts. U.S. officials in Djibouti reported that the embassy's Office of Security Cooperation, which manages U.S. security assistance for Djibouti, meets with other donors, such as Japan, France, and the European Union, on a monthly basis to discuss security assistance and identify complementary efforts.

As figure 10 illustrates, State reported considering the key factors. However, State's documentation of this consideration varied among the accounts. State documented all five key factors for two accounts (NADR/ATA and PKO), one or more of the key factors for two accounts (ESF and NADR/TIP), and none of the key factors for one account (INCLE). Therefore, State did not completely document its consideration of these factors as called for by internal control standards and its own policy manual.

Figure 10: State's Reported Consideration and Documentation of Key Factors when Selecting Partnership for Regional East Africa Counterterrorism (PREACT) Activities

Account	Country needs	Absorptive capacity	Sustainment capacity	Other U.S. efforts	Other donor efforts
NADR/ATA	●	●	●	●	●
PKO	●	●	●	●	●
ESF	●	◖	◖	●	●
NADR/TIP	●	◖	◖	◖	◖
INCLE	◖	◖	◖	◖	◖

● Considered and documented   ◖ Considered but not documented   ○ Not considered or documented

ESF   Economic Support Fund
INCLE   International Narcotics Control and Law Enforcement
NADR   Nonproliferation, Antiterrorism, Demining, and Related Programs
        ATA   Antiterrorism Assistance
        TIP   Terrorist Interdiction Program
PKO   Peacekeeping Operations

Source: GAO analysis of State Department information. | GAO-14-502

- *State documented all five key factors for NADR/ATA and PKO activities.* For NADR/ATA, State uses a standardized, formal process to conduct in-country assessments for each country that documented its consideration of all the key factors we reviewed. These assessments describe and assess partner countries' needs, absorptive capacity, and sustainment capacity. For example, in Uganda, the written ATA assessment identified border security, investigations, and critical incident management as areas that could benefit from additional ATA assistance. Likewise, a 2012 assessment documented that Tanzanian officials had demonstrated their absorptive capacity by incorporating the ATA curriculum at their academies. The most recent round of assessment reports also included standard annexes on other U.S. efforts and other donor efforts. For PKO, State selects activities from among AFRICOM proposals that provide information on, and documented consideration of, all the key factors we reviewed. AFRICOM has a formal process for developing proposals, with formal guidelines, a two-stage proposal form, and two interagency reviews. The proposal form template requests information on all five key factors. For example, in a proposal to provide Burundi with small unmanned aircraft systems, the proposal described Burundi's need for this equipment to conduct intelligence and reconnaissance operations. It also noted Burundi's lack of trained operators, addressing Burundi's absorptive capacity. The form specifically requests information on how the proposed assistance will be sustained by the recipient country or the United States. The proposal form also provides information on other U.S. and other donor efforts by collecting information on whether the proposed activity complements other ongoing initiatives in the country or region.

- *State documented three of the five key factors for activities selected for ESF funding.* The Bureau of African Affairs' proposal form for ESF activities documented consideration of partner country needs, other related U.S. efforts, and other donor efforts, but the bureau did not document its consideration of the two other key factors. The proposal form includes a section requesting information on coordination with U.S. government efforts and other donor efforts. In addition, completed proposals we reviewed included information on partner country needs. However, the proposal form does not include sections on absorptive capacity or sustainment capacity. Therefore, we were unable to verify whether Bureau of African Affairs officials had documented information about the other two key factors as they made decisions. Officials at the U.S. Embassy in Kampala reported that a PREACT-funded ESF project on social media had to be modified because the target audience did not have access to the Internet. This absorptive capacity issue may have been anticipated if State consistently documented relevant information.

- *State documented one of the five key factors for activities funded through NADR/TIP.* Officials from State's Bureau of Counterterrorism said the bureau decides which PREACT partners would receive PREACT assistance using uniform criteria. State documented its consideration of partner country needs when selecting PREACT activities through memorandums of intent and operational readiness reviews. For example, operational readiness reviews identified locations in partner countries that needed upgraded systems. However, State had no documentation of its consideration of the other four key factors.

- *State had no documentation regarding the key factors for activities funded through INCLE.* While INL reported considering the key factors through in-country visits to develop PREACT activities funded through INCLE, INL did not document these visits. According to State, INL has encountered implementation issues in trying to establish a legal adviser in Burundi because of the partner country's inability to absorb INCLE assistance. Without documentation of the in-country visits, it is unclear whether State considered Burundi's absorptive capacity before initiating this PREACT activity. As a result, State has decided to move the legal adviser to Uganda instead. This issue may have been anticipated if State consistently documented information on absorptive capacity.

State Does Not Routinely Collect and Lacks Comprehensive Information on PREACT Activities and Funding

As stated earlier, State's Bureau of African Affairs is responsible for managing PREACT and works with other bureaus and agencies to implement PREACT activities. However, the bureau does not routinely collect complete operational and financial information on PREACT that would inform decision making and ensure the effective use of resources. The *Standards for Internal Control in the Federal Government* recommends that program managers need both operational and financial data to determine whether they are meeting their agencies' plans and goals for effective and efficient use of resources.[29] While bureau officials use several methods to collect information about U.S. counterterrorism-related activities, the bureau does not have a comprehensive list of

---

[29]GAO/AIMD-00-21.3.1, 19.

PREACT-specific activities and has presented some information inaccurately in the bureau's *Performance Plans and Reports*. Similarly, the bureau uses some financial information to manage PREACT, but also does not routinely collect important financial information that could inform decision making. As a result, the bureau's reports on PREACT contained inaccuracies and may have missed opportunities to ensure PREACT funds were used to support PREACT partners.

Information Regarding PREACT Activities Is Incomplete and Reported Inaccurately in Its Annual Performance Plan and Report

The Bureau of African Affairs uses several methods to collect information about U.S. counterterrorism-related activities in East Africa. However, the bureau lacks a comprehensive list of PREACT-specific activities and has presented information regarding PREACT inaccurately in reports to senior policy officials. The *Foreign Affairs Manual* states that managers are responsible for maintaining and monitoring systems of internal controls in their areas to provide reasonable assurance that activities are carried out to further management objectives.[30] Further, the *Standards for Internal Controls in the Federal Government* states that program managers need operational data to determine if they are meeting agency goals regarding the effective use of resources.[31]

The Bureau of African Affairs has some tools in place to monitor PREACT activities. One way the bureau manages PREACT activities is by convening a routine working group with relevant State bureaus and U.S. agencies. State officials reported that the working group is a useful tool to determine what activities are being implemented and to identify any issues that need to be addressed. In addition, officials from implementing units also reported providing status updates on activities through frequent e-mail or telephone contact. AFRICOM also provides the bureau with a regular update on its PREACT activities.

The Bureau of African Affairs reports tracking counterterrorism efforts in East Africa; however, the bureau does not track separately or identify which activities included in its report were funded through PREACT and which activities were funded with other counterterrorism assistance. Because of this, the Bureau of African Affairs, which manages PREACT, did not have a distinct list of PREACT activities. As a result, it is unclear whether the Bureau of African Affairs has the ability to monitor all

---

[30]State, *Foreign Affairs Manual,* 2 FAM 022.12.

[31]GAO/AIMD-00-21.3.1, 19.

PREACT-funded activities. For example, State data indicated that ATA funds designated for PREACT were used for activities in Mauritius, which is not a PREACT partner country.[32] State officials said the allocation of funds to Mauritius was an oversight. Officials from the Bureau of African Affairs stated that each of the implementing partners (such as other State bureaus, USAID, or DOD) tracks activity information separately. However, in our attempt to obtain or compile lists of PREACT activities during the course of our 11-month review from those partners and State's Bureau of African Affairs, neither we nor State could produce a comprehensive list of activities. State's Bureau of Diplomatic Security was able to provide only a list of PREACT-funded ATA activities for 2013.

During the course of our review, we identified inaccuracies in how the Bureau of African Affairs reported on PREACT in its annual Performance Plan and Report for fiscal years 2011 and 2012, which State officials said were provided to senior U.S. policy officials and were used to inform State in reporting to Congress. In its fiscal year 2011 report, the bureau listed accounts supporting PREACT activities, but omitted ESF despite allocating funds for activities that year. For fiscal years 2011 and 2012, the bureau reported that PREACT supported counterterrorism-financing efforts in Kenya and Tanzania through NADR/Countering Terrorist Financing funds. However, information provided by State, State's Congressional Budget Justifications for fiscal year 2012, and spend plans submitted to Congress do not record NADR/Countering Terrorist Financing as an account funding PREACT activities.[33] Furthermore, in the Performance Plan and Report for fiscal year 2012, the Bureau of African Affairs reported that ATA had implemented PREACT activities in Kenya using NADR funds. However, State's Bureau of Diplomatic Security stated that it implemented ATA trainings in Kenya bilaterally and not through PREACT.[34] Other information provided by State also indicated that Kenya did not receive any PREACT-designated funds for ATA training in fiscal year 2012. We believe several of these mistakes were

---

[32] In fiscal year 2010, State provided ATA funding designated for PREACT for cyber forensics training and equipment for security forces in Mauritius, according to an official.

[33] Officials from State, Treasury, and the Department of Justice reported that their countering terrorist financing activities in the region were not formally part of PREACT, though these activities did further PREACT goals.

[34] According to State officials, Kenya may have benefitted from some PREACT regional activities supported by NADR/ATA funds. However, the *Performance Plan and Report* does not reference any regional activities.

the result of not routinely collecting data specifically on PREACT activities.

State Lacks PREACT-Specific Financial Information to Inform Decision Making

While the Bureau of African Affairs tracks allocations, it does not collect or have complete and ready access to information on the status of funds for PREACT activities that could inform decision making, including information on any unobligated balances, unliquidated obligations, and disbursements that could help inform future funding and program decisions. State's *Foreign Affairs Manual* and the *Standards for Internal Controls in the Federal Government*, call for financial reporting to help inform program decision making. The *Foreign Affairs Manual* section on Financial Management Policy states financial information is required for internal management regarding planning, programming, budgeting, performance evaluation, and reporting, and calls for the development of accurate and useful reports for internal and external use.[35] Further, the Standards for Internal Controls in the Federal Government states that financial information is required on a day-to-day basis to make operating decisions, monitor performance, and allocate resources.[36]

The Bureau of African Affairs and State's Office of Foreign Assistance Resources track allocations of funds for PREACT, while implementing bureaus and agencies, such as the Bureau for Counterterrorism, USAID, or DOD, track the status of funds. State officials reported that U.S. missions in East Africa also track the status of funds. Officials from implementing units reported providing status updates through frequent e-mail or telephone contact and through the PREACT working group. However, the Bureau of African Affairs does not consistently collect information on the status of funds, such as unobligated balances, unliquidated obligations, and disbursements. Therefore, we found that the bureau was unaware of unobligated balances and unliquidated obligations for some accounts. For example, the Bureau of African Affairs, in response to our data request, originally reported that all PREACT allocations from fiscal years 2009 to 2012 were obligated. However, after reviewing data from the implementing agencies, the bureau identified unobligated balances from the funds allocated for PREACT from NADR/ATA in prior years. State officials from the Bureaus of African Affairs and Counterterrorism stated that they had not been aware of

[35]State, *Foreign Affairs Manual,* 4 FAM 013 a.1 and 4 FAM 013 b.9.

[36]GAO/AIMD-00-21.3.1, 19.

unobligated balances in the NADR/ATA account designated for PREACT. The Bureau of African Affairs, in consultation with the Bureau for Counterterrorism and the Office of Foreign Assistance Resources, has requested higher amounts of ATA for PREACT each year since fiscal year 2011, even though there were unobligated balances from prior fiscal years totaling more than $3 million.[37] As a result, the Bureau of African Affairs made resource allocation decisions without full information on the fiscal status of available funds. Having complete and ready access to financial information, as called for by State's own *Foreign Affairs Manual* and the *Standards for Internal Controls in the Federal Government*, may have prevented the inaccuracies in bureau reporting described earlier.

Conclusions

The *U.S. National Strategy for Counterterrorism* highlights East Africa as a region of particular concern for terrorism because of al Shabaab and the al Qaeda-affiliated network's growing threat to U.S. interests that has been emanating from safe havens in the region. In addition, the President has highlighted the U.S. government's increased focus on building partner countries' capacity to combat terrorism and share the costs of common security challenges. State, in concert with other agencies, such as DOD and USAID, implements PREACT as an additional tool to further U.S. strategic objectives by allocating over $100 million since 2009 for PREACT activities to enhance partner countries' counterterrorism capabilities in East Africa.

While the PREACT initiative has funded counterterrorism assistance to foreign partners, State's Bureau of African Affairs could improve its management of the PREACT program in three areas. First, while the bureau considers partner country needs, absorptive capacity, sustainment capacity, other U.S. efforts, and other donor efforts when it selects PREACT activities, State does not fully document its consideration of these factors. Fully documenting its consideration and evaluation of these factors could enhance the transparency of the decision-making process, assist future program managers and decision makers, and provide additional assurance that resources are being efficiently allocated. Second, despite the bureau's efforts to track U.S. counterterrorism assistance in East Africa, it lacks a comprehensive list of

---

[37]These funds were requested in fiscal years 2009 through 2012 and are no longer available for new obligations.

specific PREACT activities. Improving the collection and reporting of information on PREACT activities could strengthen PREACT's whole-of-government approach to counterterrorism by ensuring all agencies have a common understanding of the activities that are being implemented. In addition, a comprehensive list of PREACT activities could help State program managers accurately assess whether the program is taking steps to achieve its goals and may help ensure there is no unnecessary duplication, overlap, or fragmentation. Third, the Bureau of African Affairs, which manages PREACT, lacks full insight into the status of the funds for PREACT activities it oversees. Collecting such information could help PREACT managers make more informed decisions about future opportunities to direct resources where they can be most effectively used, as well as improve the accuracy of its reporting. Given the ongoing threat of terrorism in East Africa, improving PREACT program management to help guide PREACT activities and target PREACT resources is essential to strengthening the partnership and making effective use of U.S. assistance in the region.

Recommendations for Executive Action

GAO recommends that the Secretary of State take the following three actions to improve the management of PREACT:

1. take steps to improve documentation of consideration of key factors when selecting PREACT activities for each funding account, such as country needs, absorptive capacity, sustainment capacity, other U.S. efforts, and other donor efforts;

2. routinely collect information on and maintain a comprehensive list of PREACT activities; and

3. routinely collect and maintain information that will better enable State to more efficiently determine and report on the status of funds allocated for PREACT.

Agency Comments and Our Evaluation

We provided a draft of this report to the Departments of State, Defense, Homeland Security, Justice, and the Treasury; to USAID; and to the Office of the Director of National Intelligence for their review and comment. State provided written comments, which we have reproduced in appendix III. State, the Department of the Treasury, and the Office of the Director of National Intelligence also provided technical comments, which we have incorporated as appropriate. The Departments of Defense, Homeland Security, and Justice, and USAID did not provide comments.

In its written comments, State concurred with all three of our recommendations to improve the management of PREACT and stated that it is taking actions to address them. More specifically, to improve its documentation of key factors considered when selecting PREACT activities, State reported that the Bureau of African Affairs is creating a streamlined reporting mechanism in line with our recommendation to improve documentation of its consideration of key factors. To collect information about and maintain a comprehensive list of PREACT activities, State is taking actions to institutionalize a working document used by the Bureau of African Affairs that currently does not differentiate between PREACT and other counterterrorism activities. Lastly, to collect and maintain information on the status of funds allocated for PREACT, State is seeking to identify better mechanisms and processes regarding financial data on PREACT activities.

We are sending copies of this report to the appropriate congressional committees; the Secretaries of State, Defense, Homeland Security, and the Treasury; the Attorney General of the United States; the Administrator of USAID; the Director of National Intelligence; and other interested parties. In addition, the report is available at no charge on the GAO website at http://www.gao.gov.

If you or your staff have any questions about this report, please contact me at (202) 512-7331 or johnsoncm@gao.gov. Contact points for our Offices of Congressional Relations and Public Affairs may be found on the last page of this report. GAO staff who made key contributions to this report are listed in appendix IV.

Charles Michael Johnson, Jr.
Director, International Affairs and Trade

Appendix I: Objectives, Scope, and Methodology

For this review of the Partnership for Regional East Africa Counterterrorism (PREACT), our objectives were to examine (1) the role PREACT plays in U.S. counterterrorism assistance to East Africa, (2) the extent to which funds allocated for PREACT since 2009 have been disbursed, and (3) the extent to which PREACT decision-making processes consider key factors and other information to inform program management.

To support our work for all three objectives, we reviewed agency documents from the Departments of State (State), Defense (DOD), Justice, the Treasury, and Homeland Security, and the U.S. Agency for International Development (USAID). We interviewed U.S. officials from those agencies in Washington, D.C.; at the U.S. Africa Command (AFRICOM) in Germany; and at U.S. missions (via video-teleconference) in Djibouti, Ethiopia, and Uganda. We selected these countries because they were among the top four recipients of PREACT funding, and collectively they implemented activities funded by all four accounts used for PREACT. We also met with officials from the Office of the Director of National Intelligence.

To examine the role PREACT plays in U.S. counterterrorism assistance to East Africa, we reviewed national, agency, and program strategic plans, including the 2011 and 2013 versions of the PREACT strategy. We examined information regarding PREACT activities from implementing entities including AFRICOM; USAID; and State's Bureaus of Counterterrorism, Diplomatic Security, International Narcotics and Law Enforcement Affairs, and Political-Military Affairs, and compared them against PREACT goals. We interviewed agency officials from State; DOD; USAID; and the Departments of the Treasury, Justice, and Homeland Security regarding what role PREACT plays in the overall U.S. counterterrorism assistance to East Africa, including efforts in Somalia. To calculate the amount allocated for other counterterrorism assistance in East Africa, we collected allocation data from State, DOD, and USAID and reviewed State's Congressional Budget Justifications.[1]

---

[1]For the purposes of this report, "other counterterrorism assistance" includes those activities funded by the U.S. government that support PREACT's goals, but were not funded using PREACT-designated money. U.S. military operations, law enforcement investigations, and intelligence activities are not included. State provided data on assistance provided to Somalia that support PREACT's counterterrorism goals.

To determine the extent to which funds allocated for PREACT have been disbursed and the amounts of unobligated balances and unliquidated obligations, we collected data from State on the status of funds used for PREACT activities for fiscal years 2009 through 2013. To assess the reliability of the data provided, we reviewed information from agency officials regarding the underlying financial data systems and the checks, controls, and reviews used to generate the data and ensure their accuracy and reliability. We found the data sufficiently reliable for our purposes. We reviewed agency documents from State, DOD, and USAID to corroborate financial data. For example, we reviewed interagency agreements and associated amendments between State and DOD regarding the implementation of Peacekeeping Operations funds for fiscal years 2010 through 2013. We also used State's Congressional Budget Justifications to corroborate State information. We analyzed data provided by State and other agencies to identify trends related to the fiscal status of PREACT funds.

To assess the extent to which PREACT decision-making processes consider key factors and other information to inform program management, we reviewed agency documents and interviewed agency officials. We reviewed the presidential policy directive on security sector assistance, which identified five key factors to be considered for assistance programs like PREACT because they are critical to building partner counterterrorism capacity and to focusing limited resources: country needs, absorptive capacity, sustainment capacity, other U.S. efforts, and other donor efforts. To determine the extent to which State considered and documented those factors when selecting activities to implement with PREACT funds, we reviewed agency guidance, country assessments, proposal forms, and implementation agreements. For example, we analyzed assessments conducted by the Bureau of Diplomatic Security's Antiterrorism Assistance program of Burundi, Djibouti, Ethiopia, Kenya, Somalia, Tanzania, and Uganda from 2010 through 2012. We traveled to Germany to meet with AFRICOM officials and gather information about AFRICOM's role in collecting and sharing information with State on the key factors. We also interviewed U.S. officials from State's Bureaus of African Affairs, Counterterrorism, Diplomatic Security, International Narcotics and Law Enforcement Affairs, and Political-Military Affairs; DOD; and USAID in Washington, D.C., and officials at AFRICOM and U.S. missions in East Africa to obtain their perspectives on how they considered key factors when selecting PREACT activities.

To understand what information was used to manage the implementation of PREACT activities, we compared activity and financial information, when available, regarding PREACT activities provided by State's Bureau of African Affairs—which manages PREACT—with information provided by the implementing entities including AFRICOM; USAID; and State's Bureaus of Counterterrorism, Diplomatic Security, and Political-Military Affairs. We also reviewed how the Bureau of African Affairs reported on PREACT activities in its annual *Performance Plan and Report* for fiscal years 2009-2012. In addition, we interviewed U.S. officials from State's Bureaus of African Affairs, Counterterrorism, International Narcotics and Law Enforcement Affairs, and Political-Military Affairs and USAID in Washington, D.C., and officials at AFRICOM and U.S. missions in East Africa to gather information about implementation of PREACT activities in partner countries and the extent to which U.S. officials in the field gather information on the key factors, status of implementation, and status of funding and provide that information to decision makers in Washington.

We conducted this performance audit from July 2013 to June 2014 in accordance with generally accepted government auditing standards. Those standards require that we plan and perform the audit to obtain sufficient, appropriate evidence to provide a reasonable basis for our findings and conclusions based on our audit objectives. We believe the evidence obtained provides a reasonable basis for our findings and conclusions based on our audit objectives.

Appendix II: Status of Partnership for Regional East Africa Counterterrorism Funds

The information below describes, by account, the status of funds allocated for the Partnership for Regional East Africa Counterterrorism (PREACT), as of November 2013. The tables show unobligated balances—which are the portions of allocations that have not yet been obligated—and unliquidated obligations—which are the amounts of obligations incurred for which payment has not yet been made.

State allocates funding for PREACT activities through the following four accounts: Economic Support Fund (ESF); Peacekeeping Operations (PKO); International Narcotics Control and Law Enforcement (INCLE); and Nonproliferation, Antiterrorism, Demining, and Related Programs (NADR). State's Bureau of African Affairs manages the PREACT program overall; however other State bureaus lead the design and selection of PREACT activities funded from the various accounts.

Status of ESF Account Funds Allocated for PREACT Activities

State's Bureau of African Affairs leads the design and selection of PREACT activities funded by ESF. As table 3 shows, for fiscal years 2009 through 2013, State allocated about $8.4 million for ESF. It allocated the largest amounts of its ESF funds for PREACT activities in Kenya to promote democratic participation and in Somalia to engage Somali populations. As of November 2013, State had obligated all ESF funds appropriated for fiscal year 2012 and earlier. State officials explained that the agency had not yet obligated funds that Congress appropriated for fiscal year 2013 for implementation in specific countries or activities, and these funds remain available for obligation until September 30, 2014. State had disbursed about half of the approximately $8.4 million of ESF funding for PREACT activities as of November 2013.

Table 3: Economic Support Fund (ESF) Funding Allocated and Disbursed, by Fiscal Year Appropriated, toward Partnership for Regional East Africa Counterterrorism (PREACT) Activities in Partner Countries, as of November 2013

Dollars in thousands

	2009	2010	2011	2012	2013	Total
Allocated	-	2,500	2,039	2,000	1,900	**8,439**
Unobligated balance	-	0	0	0	1,900[a]	**1,900**
Unliquidated obligations	-	334	250	1,193	0	**1,777**
Disbursed	-	2,166	1,789	807	0	**4,762**

Source: GAO analysis of State Department data. | GAO-14-502

Notes: The amounts above reflect funds dedicated for PREACT activities appropriated by fiscal year.

[a]This unobligated balance reflects fiscal year 2013 appropriations that remain available for obligation until September 30, 2014, and State is in the process of obligating these funds.

Status of PKO Account Funds Allocated for PREACT Activities

State's Bureau of Political-Military Affairs leads the design and selection of PREACT activities funded by PKO. As table 4 shows, for fiscal years 2009 through 2013, State allocated about $45 million for PKO. State had obligated all PKO funds to support activities in partner countries as of November 2013. While State had disbursed about $8 million (or 18 percent) of PKO funds as of November 2013, unliquidated obligations account for more than half of the PKO allocations every fiscal year since 2009. However, after the period of availability for obligation has ended, U.S. agencies have an additional 5 years to disburse those funds. Therefore, no PKO funds allocated for PREACT activities had expired as of November 2013.

Table 4: Peacekeeping Operations (PKO) Funding Allocated and Disbursed, by Fiscal Year Appropriated, toward Partnership for Regional East Africa Counterterrorism (PREACT) Activities in Partner Countries, as of November 2013

Dollars in thousands

	2009	2010	2011	2012	2013	Total
Allocated	5,000	10,000	9,960	10,000	10,000	**44,960**
Unobligated balance	0	0	0	0	0	**0**
Unliquidated obligations	2,827	6,371	8,497	9,307	9,986	**36,988**
Disbursed	2,173	3,629	1,463	693	14	**7,972**

Source: GAO analysis of State Department data. | GAO-14-502

Note: The amounts above reflect funds dedicated for PREACT activities appropriated by fiscal year.

Status of INCLE Account Funds Allocated for PREACT Activities

State's Bureau for International Narcotics and Law Enforcement Affairs leads the design and selection of PREACT activities funded by INCLE. As table 5 shows, State allocated a total of $6 million in INCLE funds under PREACT in fiscal years 2010, 2012, and 2013. State had allocated these funds for Burundi, Somalia, Tanzania, Uganda, and regional activities. As of November 2013, State had obligated all INCLE funds appropriated for fiscal year 2012 and earlier. State officials explained that the agency had not yet obligated funds that Congress appropriated for fiscal year 2013 for implementation in specific countries or activities, and these funds remain available for obligation until September 30, 2014. State had disbursed $682,000 (or 11 percent) of INCLE funds allocated, as of November 2013. In addition, State officials reported that they had encountered challenges implementing the INCLE program in Burundi and amended the program to be based in Uganda.

Table 5: International Narcotics Control and Law Enforcement Affairs (INCLE) Funding Allocated and Disbursed, by Fiscal Year Appropriated, toward Partnership for Regional East Africa Counterterrorism (PREACT) Activities in Partner Countries, as of November 2013

Dollars in thousands

	2009	2010	2011	2012	2013	Total
Allocated	-	2,000	-	2,000	2,000	**6,000**
Unobligated balance	-	0	-	0	2,000[a]	**2,000**
Unliquidated obligations	-	1,634	-	1,684	0	**3,318**
Disbursed	-	366	-	316	0	**682**

Source: GAO analysis of State Department data. | GAO-14-502

Notes: The amounts above reflect funds dedicated for PREACT activities appropriated by fiscal year.

[a]This unobligated balance reflects fiscal year 2013 appropriations that remain available for obligation until September 30, 2014, and State is in the process of obligating these funds.

Status of NADR Account Funds Allocated for PREACT Activities

State's Bureau of Counterterrorism leads the design and selection of PREACT activities funded by NADR. For fiscal years 2009 through 2013, State allocated a total of about $44.6 million in NADR funds to support PREACT activities in East African countries. State split this assistance between the Antiterrorism Assistance program (ATA) and the Terrorist Interdiction Program (TIP).

As shown in table 6, about $34.3 million had been allocated for NADR/ATA activities. State had disbursed about $19.8 million (or 58 percent) of the NADR/ATA allocated funds as of November 2013. State carried an unobligated balance for each fiscal year as of November 2013. The majority of the unobligated balance ($8.5 million, or 73 percent) is from fiscal year 2013 because State is in the process of obligating those funds, which remain available for obligation until September 30, 2014. For funds allocated in fiscal year 2012 and earlier, State has about $3.1 million in unobligated balances. State has either 1 or 2 years to obligate NADR funds, depending on the purpose for which the NADR funds are appropriated. Therefore, the authority to incur new obligations for any funds appropriated in fiscal year 2012 and earlier that were not obligated has expired. These unobligated balances remain available for an additional 5 fiscal years for recording and adjusting obligations properly chargeable to the appropriation's period of availability. For example, these funds may remain available for contract modifications properly within the scope of the original contract. Officials from State's Bureaus of Diplomatic Security and Counterterrorism acknowledged that about $3.1 million in NADR/ATA funds remains unobligated and is no longer available for new obligations. Despite having unobligated balances from prior fiscal years, State has requested higher amounts of ATA for PREACT each year since fiscal year 2011, requesting more than $9 million for fiscal year 2014.

Table 6: Nonproliferation, Antiterrorism, Demining, and Related Programs (NADR) Funding for Antiterrorism Assistance (ATA) Allocated and Disbursed, by Fiscal Year Appropriated, toward Partnership for Regional East Africa Counterterrorism (PREACT) Activities in Partner Countries, as of November 2013

Dollars in thousands

	2009	2010	2011	2012	2013	Total
Allocated	3,781	7,578	6,948	7,472	8,537	**34,316**
Unobligated balance	829[a]	881[a]	532[a]	871[a]	8,537[b]	**11,650**
Unliquidated obligations	64	474	389	1,990	0	**2,917**
Disbursed	2,888	6,223	6,028	4,611	0	**19,750**

Source: GAO analysis of State Department data. | GAO-14-502

Notes: The amounts above reflect funds dedicated for PREACT activities appropriated by fiscal year.

[a]According to State officials, the period of availability to incur new obligations has expired for these unobligated balances. These unobligated balances remain available for an additional 5 fiscal years for recording and adjusting obligations properly chargeable to the appropriation's period of availability. For example, these funds may remain available for contract modifications properly within the scope of the original contract.

[b]This unobligated balance reflects fiscal year 2013 appropriations that remain available for obligation until September 30, 2014, and State is in the process of obligating these funds.

As shown in table 7, State had allocated a total of about $10.3 million for NADR/TIP activities for fiscal years 2009 through 2013. As of November 2013, State had obligated and disbursed all funds allocated for TIP activities from fiscal years 2009 through 2012.

Table 7: Nonproliferation, Antiterrorism, Demining, and Related Programs (NADR) Funding for Terrorist Interdiction Program (TIP) Allocated and Disbursed, by Fiscal Year Appropriated, toward Partnership for Regional East Africa Counterterrorism (PREACT) Activities in Partner Countries, as of November 2013

Dollars in thousands

	2009	2010	2011	2012	2013	Total
Allocated	2,700	2,570	2,000	1,850	1,161	**10,281**
Unobligated balance	0	0	0	0	1,161[a]	**1,161**
Unliquidated obligations	0	0	0	0	0	**0**
Disbursed	2,700	2,570	2,000	1,850	0	**9,120**

Source: GAO analysis of State Department data. | GAO-14-502

Note: The amounts above reflect funds dedicated for PREACT activities appropriated by fiscal year.

[a]This unobligated balance reflects fiscal year 2013 appropriations that remain available for obligation until September 30, 2014, and State is in the process of obligating these funds.

Appendix III: Comments from the Department of State

Note: GAO comments supplementing those in the report text appear at the end of this appendix.

United States Department of State
Comptroller
P.O. Box 150008
Charleston, SC 29415-5008

JUN ‾2 2014

Dr. Loren Yager
Managing Director
International Affairs and Trade
Government Accountability Office
441 G Street, N.W.
Washington, D.C. 20548-0001

Dear Dr. Yager:

We appreciate the opportunity to review your draft report, "COMBATING TERRORISM: State Department Can Improve Management of East Africa Program" GAO Job Code 320987.

The enclosed Department of State comments are provided for incorporation with this letter as an appendix to the final report.

If you have any questions concerning this response, please contact Peter Quaranto, Counterterrorism Officer, Bureau of African Affairs at (202) 736-4435.

Sincerely,

Christopher H. Flaggs, Acting

Enclosure: as stated.

cc: GAO – Charles Michael Johnson
     AF – Linda Thomas-Greenfield
     State/OIG – Norman Brown

Department of State Comments on GAO Draft Report

<u>**COMBATING TERRORISM: State Department Can Improve Management
of East Africa Program**</u>
(GAO-14-502, GAO Code 320987)

Thank you for allowing the Department of State the opportunity to comment
on the draft report, *"COMBATING TERRORISM: State Department Can Improve
Management of East Africa Program."* The Department deeply appreciates the
professionalism of the GAO team over the course of this yearlong project, and the
thoughtfulness and sensitivity they demonstrated in carrying out their duties.

The Department of State is committed to working with other U.S. agencies
and international partners to build the capacity and resilience of governments and
civil society to contain the spread of, and ultimately counter the threat posed by al-
Qa'ida, al-Shabaab, and other violent extremist organizations in East Africa. As
highlighted in GAO's report, we view the Partnership for Regional East Africa
Counterterrorism (PREACT) as a valuable tool in this regard. PREACT provides
dedicated, flexible funding that enables multi-year planning. Furthermore, as
GAO's report notes, "The regional nature of PREACT encourages implementing
agencies to view counterterrorism from a regional perspective, rather than country-
by-country." We appreciate that the GAO report highlights these strengths,
although we are disappointed that they are not included in the GAO report's
Executive Summary.

See comment 1.

Over the past year, we have taken a number of steps to strengthen PREACT
and implement key practices of interagency collaboration. These include (1)
agreeing on an updated joint, interagency strategy to guide PREACT activities; (2)
institutionalizing the interagency PREACT Working Group, which holds monthly
meetings and/or teleconferences; (3) setting up an email listserv to enable better
information-sharing among PREACT implementing agencies and stakeholders;
and (4) establishing an annual strategic planning process involving U.S. embassies
to validate PREACT's priorities and evaluate its overall progress. We have also
taken steps to improve coordination with international partners, including through
the Global Counterterrorism Forum's Horn of Africa Working Group. We regret
that these steps were not more significantly highlighted in GAO's report.

See comment 2.

The GAO report's first recommendation is that the Department of State take
steps to improve documentation of the consideration of key factors such as country
needs, absorptive capacity, sustainment capacity, other U.S. efforts, and other

-2-

donor efforts when selecting PREACT program activities. The GAO report rightly
assesses that these factors are considered in most programmatic decisions, but we
agree that it is important to have consistent, centralized documentation of this
consideration. While the number of implementing units and U.S. embassies
involved in PREACT poses coordination challenges, the Bureau of African Affairs
is working to establish improved, streamlined reporting mechanisms in line with
GAO's recommendation. We note, however, that additional staffing would be
required to fully address this recommendation.

The GAO report's second recommendation is that the Department of State
routinely collect and maintain a comprehensive list of PREACT activities. The
Bureau of African Affairs already maintains a working document that provides a
comprehensive list of PREACT and related counterterrorism activities, which is
regularly updated by the interagency PREACT Working Group. We believe it is
important to include related activities in this document (e.g., global
counterterrorism funding allocated to East Africa, such as the Department of
Defense's Section 1206 funding for training and equipping military forces) to
ensure that all relevant efforts are coordinated and aligned. Nevertheless, we agree
with GAO that is important to formalize and institutionalize this document so it is
easier to share a comprehensive list of PREACT activities with key stakeholders.
We will take actions to that end.

Finally, the GAO report's third recommendation is that the Department of
State routinely collect and maintain information that will better enable State to
more efficiently determine and report on the status of funds allocated for PREACT.
The report notes that while this information is collected and analyzed by the
respective implementing units, it is not consistently and comprehensively provided
to the Bureau of African Affairs. We agree with GAO that this is an area for
improvement. The number of implementing units and U.S. embassies involved,
each with their own reporting chains and requirements – as well as staff limitations
within the Bureau – poses considerable challenges in this regard, but we are
seeking to identify better mechanisms and processes for collecting and maintaining
financial data on PREACT activities.

Again, the Department of State expresses our sincere thanks to the GAO for
its thoughtful assessments and engagement throughout this process. Please be
assured that the Department takes the GAO's findings very seriously and will
continue to work to strengthen PREACT and all other tools that can advance our
counterterrorism efforts in East Africa.

The following are GAO's comments on the Department of State's letter dated June 2, 2014.

GAO Comments

1. In GAO's Highlights of this report, we note the amount of funding allocated for regional activities.

2. While interagency collaboration was not the focus of our review, we note on page 29 that the Bureau of African Affairs convenes a PREACT working group and uses email to monitor PREACT activities. We have also incorporated some information regarding State's recently-developed PREACT strategic plan and strategic planning process.

Appendix IV: GAO Contact and Staff Acknowledgments

GAO Contact

Charles Michael Johnson, Jr., (202) 512-7331 or johnsoncm@gao.gov

Staff Acknowledgments

In addition to the contact named above, Jason L. Bair (Assistant Director), Miriam Carroll Fenton, and Brandon L. Hunt made key contributions to this report. Ashley Alley, Martin de Alteriis, Karen Deans, and Etana Finkler provided technical assistance.

Related GAO Products

Afghanistan: Oversight and Accountability of U.S. Assistance. GAO-14-680T. Washington, D.C.: June 10, 2014.

Countering Overseas Threats: DOD and State Need to Address Gaps in Monitoring of Security Equipment Transferred to Lebanon. GAO-14-161. Washington, D.C.: February 26, 2014.

Central America: U.S. Agencies Considered Various Factors in Funding Security Activities, but Need to Assess Progress in Achieving Interagency Objectives. GAO-13-771. Washington, D.C.: September 25, 2013.

Combating Terrorism: DHS Should Take Action to Better Ensure Resources Abroad Align with Priorities. GAO-13-681. Washington, D.C.: September 25, 2013.

Building Partner Capacity: DOD is Meeting Most Targets for Colombia's Regional Helicopter Training Center but Should Track Graduates. GAO-13-674. Washington, D.C.: July 24, 2013.

Status of Funding, Equipment, and Training for the Caribbean Basin Security Initiative. GAO-13-367R. Washington, D.C.: March 20, 2013.

U.S. Assistance to Yemen: Actions Needed to Improve Oversight of Emergency Food Aid and Assess Security Assistance. GAO-13-310. Washington, D.C.: March 20, 2013.

Building Partner Capacity: Key Practices to Effectively Manage Department of Defense Efforts to Promote Security Cooperation. GAO-13-335T. Washington, D.C.: February 14, 2013.

Afghanistan: Key Oversight Issues. GAO-13-218SP. Washington, D.C.: February 11, 2013.

Security Force Assistance: DOD's Consideration of Unintended Consequences, Perverse Incentives, and Moral Hazards. GAO-13-241R. Washington, D.C.: January 8, 2013.

Counternarcotics Assistance: U.S. Agencies Have Allotted Billions In Andean Countries, but DOD Should Improve Its Reporting of Results. GAO-12-824. Washington, D.C.: July 10, 2012.

Combating Terrorism: State Should Enhance Its Performance Measures for Assessing Efforts in Pakistan to Counter Improvised Explosive Devices. GAO-12-614. Washington, D.C.: May 15, 2012.

Foreign Police Assistance: Defined Roles and Improved Information Sharing Could Enhance Interagency Collaboration. GAO-12-534. Washington, D.C.: May 9, 2012.

Uncertain Political and Security Situation Challenges U.S. Efforts to Implement a Comprehensive Strategy in Yemen. GAO-12-432R. Washington, D.C.: February 29, 2012.

Combating Terrorism: Additional Steps Needed to Enhance Foreign Partners' Capacity to Prevent Terrorist Travel. GAO-11-637. Washington, D.C.: June 30, 2011.

Combating Terrorism: U.S. Government Should Improve Its Reporting on Terrorist Safe Havens. GAO-11-561. Washington, D.C.: June 3, 2011.

Combating Terrorism: Planning and Documentation of U.S. Development Assistance in Pakistan's Federally Administered Tribal Areas Need to Be Improved. GAO-10-289. Washington, D.C.: April 15, 2010.

Combating Terrorism: U.S. Agencies Report Progress Countering Terrorism and Its Financing in Saudi Arabia, but Continued Focus on Counter Terrorism Financing Efforts Needed. GAO-09-883. Washington, D.C.: September 24, 2009.

Securing, Stabilizing, and Developing Pakistan's Border Area with Afghanistan: Key Issues for Congressional Oversight. GAO-09-263SP. Washington, D.C.: February 23, 2009.

Combating Terrorism: Actions Needed to Enhance Implementation of Trans-Sahara Counterterrorism Partnership. GAO-08-860. Washington, D.C.: July 31, 2008.

Somalia: Several Challenges Limit U.S. and International Stabilization, Humanitarian, and Development Efforts. GAO-08-351. Washington, D.C.: February 19, 2008.

GAO's Mission	The Government Accountability Office, the audit, evaluation, and investigative arm of Congress, exists to support Congress in meeting its constitutional responsibilities and to help improve the performance and accountability of the federal government for the American people. GAO examines the use of public funds; evaluates federal programs and policies; and provides analyses, recommendations, and other assistance to help Congress make informed oversight, policy, and funding decisions. GAO's commitment to good government is reflected in its core values of accountability, integrity, and reliability.
Obtaining Copies of GAO Reports and Testimony	The fastest and easiest way to obtain copies of GAO documents at no cost is through GAO's website (http://www.gao.gov). Each weekday afternoon, GAO posts on its website newly released reports, testimony, and correspondence. To have GAO e-mail you a list of newly posted products, go to http://www.gao.gov and select "E-mail Updates."
Order by Phone	The price of each GAO publication reflects GAO's actual cost of production and distribution and depends on the number of pages in the publication and whether the publication is printed in color or black and white. Pricing and ordering information is posted on GAO's website, http://www.gao.gov/ordering.htm. Place orders by calling (202) 512-6000, toll free (866) 801-7077, or TDD (202) 512-2537. Orders may be paid for using American Express, Discover Card, MasterCard, Visa, check, or money order. Call for additional information.
Connect with GAO	Connect with GAO on Facebook, Flickr, Twitter, and YouTube. Subscribe to our RSS Feeds or E-mail Updates. Listen to our Podcasts. Visit GAO on the web at www.gao.gov.
To Report Fraud, Waste, and Abuse in Federal Programs	Contact: Website: http://www.gao.gov/fraudnet/fraudnet.htm E-mail: fraudnet@gao.gov Automated answering system: (800) 424-5454 or (202) 512-7470
Congressional Relations	Katherine Siggerud, Managing Director, siggerudk@gao.gov, (202) 512-4400, U.S. Government Accountability Office, 441 G Street NW, Room 7125, Washington, DC 20548
Public Affairs	Chuck Young, Managing Director, youngc1@gao.gov, (202) 512-4800 U.S. Government Accountability Office, 441 G Street NW, Room 7149 Washington, DC 20548

Please Print on Recycled Paper.